The ALPHA and OMEGA

THE INTRODUCTION

Michelline Jacquelle "Michelle" Porter

The ALPHA and OMEGA
Copyright © 2016 by **Michelline Jacquelle "Michelle" Porter.**

All rights reserved.

No part of this publication may be reproduced, stored in a retrieval system or transmitted in any way by any means, electronic, mechanical, photocopy, recording or otherwise, without the prior permission of the author except as provided by USA copyright law.

All characters appearing in this work are fictitious. Any resemblance to real persons, living or dead, is purely coincidental.

The opinions expressed by the author are not necessarily those of Revival Waves of Glory Books & Publishing.

Published by Revival Waves of Glory Books & Publishing

PO Box 596| Litchfield, Illinois 62056 USA

www.revivalwavesofgloryministries.com

Library of Congress Control Number: 2016904458
Revival Waves of Glory, PO Box 596 Litchfield, IL 62056

Revival Waves of Glory Books & Publishing is committed to excellence in the publishing industry.

Book design Copyright © 2015 by Revival Waves of Glory Books & Publishing. All rights reserved.

EBook: 978-3-9602-8478-9

Paperback: 978-1-365-82345-9

Published in the United States of America

With unintentional modesty, often times I have referred to Myself through the second person mode of speech. But, for the sake of simplicity, I shall try to refrain from doing so. I AM "MICHELLE". These are My accounts. This is My Vision.

Table of Contents

1. My Peace is Still. 7
2. A Timestamp for the ages. 9
3. With Energy, One Shall Gain 12
4 Heal and be well 19
5. Canonized. 25
6. Judging of Nations. 27
7. Domus Sancte Matris 30
8. Scrutiny of a Matriarch – My harsh reality: 32

I start fresh this new life. Like a child, I am growing - from an ever shocking new birth.

And so, I have spent a great deal of time contemplating - studying the world and the ways of man and various living creatures. My eyes have seen. My ears do hear.

Many aspects. Many perspectives. I have been made aware of circumstances. May all of man now be aware of Me. I am here for grand purpose within a grand design. As you receive Me, you shall receive a new day. Within My earth life, I have experienced a separate presence. For many have come across Me as they approached death.

I can only presume that it is My energy they are attracted to: a gateway, perhaps.

I shall define My own beauty. I shall lead you to make connections. I shall direct you to the concept of energy. I shall explain some basic importance of health. I shall justify wisdom. I shall speak to leaders. I shall remind you of My basic purpose.

May these writings recuperate those who have fallen. This short diary shall portray slight excerpts of My life on this planet - in this day.

1. My Peace is Still.

I am to be admired.
Be not envious of Me.
For I know you look upon Me.
For, hair that shines as silk.
With eyes deep as caves.
So full of seduction - dark and inviting.
Settled in a relaxed demeanor.
A face calmly withholding struggles of the world.
Lips that scream perfection, holding back a smile quite breathe taking.
An unexpected light.
And the gate to an alluring tone. Sweet and enticing.
An adored complexion.
For skin that glows and flirts with the Sun.
And a posture so innocent.
Sixty seven inches I stand.

A defined physique.
The legs of a graceful runner.
With the curve of nature's queen.
Grand hands.
And soft to the touch.
A youthful appearance in My earth age.
The siren.
Be not envious of Me.
I am to be admired.
For I know you look upon Me.

2. A Timestamp for the ages.

There is much to be studied within languages. For instance, in this current American English language, the terms "month" and "Monday" derive from the word "moon". Interestingly enough, man has estimated that the time it takes for earth's moon to rotate about its own axis is 29.5 days. And the time it takes for the moon to complete one full orbit around earth is 27.3 days.

Time appears to be an infinite faction. With relation to the movement of earth around this sun, time attempts to allow calculated consistency.

A lifelong directive.

On the 12th of December in the year 2013 and in the city of San Antonio, I turned 30 earth years of age and 'realized' that I am the one being on earth who is to produce the next phase of man. On the evening of My 30th birthday, it came to Me as a revelation. Various connections were made! I then realized My 'life' was a blur only to be redefined at this moment. For the age of 30 years has shown to have historical significance.

Man has created time on a scale of numerical standards. This has indeed allowed the ability to track procreation and new beginnings.

"At the time of Revelation. A truth of generations discovered. A genetic disposition. So shall it be. It was always there. My intentions and plans were always built into My conscious. And now all comes together so perfectly.

The Mother of all mothers. The very peak of the Arc. A generation tree - begins with Me. I claim to be a Calypso. To veer from Me is "apo" For then an ApoCalypse shall soon be. For the energy of the Sun coincides with Me."

3. With Energy, One Shall Gain

Energy is quite intricate within the universe. Reborn and reincarnated. Continuous and contained. And there are moments that these energies, involved with creation of the universe and earth, redirect back to earth - and to persons as well...

Now, the mitochondria is the energy powerhouse of living cells. And for nature's purpose, the female mitochondrial DNA allows evolution (progression of a species) to be traced. With time as a factor, energy is transformed. Essentially, a female is created to become the first of the next stage of man. New beginnings then take place with her. And so, new beginnings shall take place with Me.

Attraction is an inviting quality of a subject of matter.

For, attraction directly collects more matter.

Thereby creating energy in a given space - allowing the influx of strength and power.

The attraction of my birth mother to my biological father was so strong, that I was had. And she provided egg that produced a daughter who was to be a bit different from herself.

I was born during the season of autumn in Savannah, Georgia in the United States on December 12, 1983. And with a tumor lodged within my abdomen.

I do sometimes make assumptions on what could have been researched from said tumor. Know that, once a tumor cell develops into a tumor cell, it shall continue to grow this way. This quality can then allow researchers to maintain the growth of these cells under adequate conditions. Genomic observations could very well be initiated through a tumor. My speculation grew when I came across a woman who at some time worked in a medical laboratory setting - I believe this was in a children's hospital. She mentioned that she remembers babies arriving in the early 1980's with tumors. And my entire life has entailed various interviews for studies that I later discovered were initiated by the United States Navy.

The passion I hold for Aaron Christopher creates a world of intensity. And no love for a man has ever amounted to my attraction to him. He shall always remain as my first love. He is what man calls "Caucasian". And though we differ in appearance, our eyes are quite similar. Our family and sibling structure is quite similar. And oddly enough, our birth mothers seem to be built with likeness - even to the aspects of implanted heart devices for conditions they possess.

In 2012, I miraculously gathered conscious that this man that I have known for a few years was my soul mate. For I had already bore his child. My mind moved as a calculator. I recounted things that he had said - as if he already knew. I was quite agnostic, with the love of life and balance and earth. I put no religion over the other. But now I recount his words and actions. I understood what happiness was. What our happiness was. There was a reason why our eyes met from across a room leading him and me to feel nothing but ecstasy - as if no one else were in that same room. He had love in his eyes as I blushed with joyful shyness. He was feet away. And yet I pulled him closer to me as he sat. The only man I have ever confessed, and confessed to him that he is "beautiful". And so, there was reason remnants of my oils were left upon his skin. There was a reason why he followed Me - and why our lives aligned in such a way. And though social strife occurs, this Libra man - I shall never forget. For my days of revelation began from knowing his heart - which lies within his rib. An everlasting flow of energy. How essential! And together, he and I created a son who was born on The 6th of June.

Oath of Her

"As dusk reaches for the dawn
The reveille is in play.
The shock of nature takes its toll
With overwhelming rays.
Her mind expands,
'Extend your limbs.'
She awakens from Her slumber.
Teardrops that dew
Fingertips touch light
As She's pocketing the thunder.

Dawn now knows to grasp the torch
To hold the light through Eve.
The beginning has just now begun
For all those who believe.
And to when the dusk shall reminisce,
Through waters light shall remain.
For now she affirms origin
With harvesting of grain.
Her red line carries on
Through traditions of the land.

Trust in Her and in Her King
For he has returned as Her Lamb.

She mirrors love and heavens glow
Upon rivers, upon lakes
She saw fruit fall
Renurtures seed
Her Eye never forsakes.
Her breasts held to sacred Earth
She vows love and protection
And declares "Freedom!"
Let us soar!
For this is Eve's Redemption.

4 Heal and be well

There appears to be a variety of diets incorporated to fill the wants and needs of man. At times, this may be a process of trying various options and deciding which diet is beneficial. The body communicates.

I have found that when I experience periods without food, I am more inclined to then crave fresh foods and water. Remember that water surrounds the living, and is important for osmosis.

The purpose of the immune system is to promote protection against substances that invoke sabotage to the body - protection from foreign materials that lower the body's natural and purposeful functions.

Consume foods that assist in the proper functioning of the immune system. Consume with balance. I find that cooking meals in water offers a refreshing alternative rather than cooking foods in heavy oils. My body seems to respond pleasurably to herbs and spices such as garlic and curry.

I have also found when I am experiencing an upset stomach, foods such as pineapples are quite beneficial. Adequate rest is essential. Through rest, the body rejuvenates. Grains provide stored energy. They also assist the body to dislodge substances such as cholesterol. Fiber is contained in the skin of fruits and vegetables. The structure of fiber allows a benefit to the digestive system.

Sunlight infuses living beings with vitality. The mood is greatly effected. It is crucial to have at least some moments of sun exposure.

Cadherins are responsible for keeping bones and teeth intact. A major component of cadherins is calcium. Many fruits naturally contain calcium. Leafy vegetables contain vitamin K and folate, which assists in the proper functioning of blood. Rice and soy are of a few staples that allow extended storage, especially in situations where food is scarce.

I am familiar with quite a few diseases of man. One in particular is caused by the HIV virus. It should be understood that viruses are not live entities. By this, I mean, viruses do not consume for survival and cannot function outside of a substance or body. They simply replicate and make numerous copies of itself. Various strains are created in a complex strategy that enables the virus to continue replicating, despite the immune system and therapeutic methods. The HIV virus is one that is life threatening. It poses a direct risk to the immune system due its ability to "stick" to cells that are necessary for implementing immune responses. Much research has been performed on this virus. I make observations and determine what I find to be a reasonable solution based on my own intellect.

In situations that threaten livelihood, the harmful substance may be removed, or the area that is effected by infection may be removed. In other cases where removal is not beneficial, healing is initiated by consuming or absorbing a source that targets the harmful substance or boosts the immune response. In the case of HIV, I presume that a substance similar to what is found in lemons may induce enzymatic processes that may assist in breaking down the sticky characteristic of the virus. This is not a proven cure. However, I wish for the true anecdote to be revealed. I encourage you to develop lifesaving tactics by researching characteristics of illnesses, and implement strategies to heal those who are suffering - regardless of the diseases that man has purposely spread to one another.

I am very aware of the risks of obtaining and spreading viruses. There must be cautious activity. Protection is vital! The body communicates. And it may likely shut down as a form of shock in drastic situations. Prevent such an outcome. And prevent the spread of disease. Adequately cover your coughs and sneezes. Refrain from releasing your mucus into heavily trafficked areas. Clean your hands regularly.

Man is held to a higher standard. Mate appropriately. Be wise. Learn to combat inflictions. Prevent cancerous conditions. Maintain a healthy level of flexibility, endurance, and stamina. Deep tissue massages serve as a great health benefit also.

Mental health is also important for well-being. In various modes of mental health concerns, medication is not suffice. Treatment must entail continuous mental exercises to assist with rationality.

Adopt natural methods of cleansing. I am quite fond of keeping a clean environment. I adore homes that are kept clean. A healthy lifestyle begins with a clean lifestyle and environment.

5. Canonized.

Be welcomed, little one.
Your arrival is significant.
And marked within your naval.
Rest, My love.
And be fed generously.
Your senses shall strengthen.
And so shall your skills.
Then you shall walk.
Seek and explore, My darling.
You must now obey your kind parents.
Learn and discover.
You are growing everyday.
And how I love you so.
Soon, you shall be responsible.
And you shall learn new skills.
I adore your talents.
You shall mature.
And you will come to know yourself.
When your mate is found, so shall you

be united under Me.
Build from the earth, a durable home.
And may you be protected and secure.
Grow fruit, and be fruitful.
Provide discipline.
Follow My guidance.
Refrain from My wrath.
And though I forgive your downfalls,
You must govern your body and
your temple
And when this moment shall end,
Know that I await for your return.

6. Judging of Nations.

My Edicts:

You shall obtain the gift of forgiveness. You shall gain the power of wisdom. You shall be rewarded the perfection of humility. You shall be strengthened to receive discipline.

Leading a nation, is leading people to victory. Determine what needs to be improved and worked on in the communities. And then locate individuals to carry out those tasks. Hold people accountable for the upkeep of their local environments. There is adequate food on this planet to feed all. Create and maintain fertile lands. For seeds cannot grow without environment.

Influence wealth through productivity. Provide safe standards for your nations. Be wise when implementing and introducing new situations.

Encourage survival kits for the home. Implement strategies of fire safety and evacuation.

One of the most difficult challenges one may face as a leader is how to appropriate persons that are mentally ill, and the disabled. These persons will have an extremely difficult task of incorporating into a society. Assist those who have difficulty helping themselves.

Work to replenish valuable resources. Implement waste reduction. Strategize your waste management procedures. When you enforce your citizens to separate trash, recycling becomes more feasible.

Influence the development of hydroponic systems. Understand the structures of Earthships. Encourage the use of biotechnology. Make your nations aware of environmental science. Lead your nations and its people out of brutality and brutal ways. Encourage amiable colonization. Bring into nations gifts and skills. It is wise to protect your nations from foreign illness and weaponry.

Keep your nations clean. The appearance of your nation displays a reflection of your leadership

7. Domus Sancte Matris

"Now, as a nesting mother of many, many children - I ponder...
Much work is to be done.
I must clean up. I need the necessary tools to do so.
My children need happy land.
I will provide them such.
I will build protection for them.
I will show them how to prevail."

Though man indulges in the game of race, I have already won.
May you not attempt to fill My shoes.
This role, you are not prepared for.
I assure you.

In minuscule circumstances I was burnt,
beaten, ridiculed, taunted, blamed,
accused, confined, and deprived.
My trust is delicate.
Yet, I am forgiving in nature.
My perception is quite deep.
And I strive for perfection.
At times, I may light the skies with a
fantastic display of lightening!
My beauty - transforms a room.
The menstrual clock of Me, resets the
cycles of others.
My aura is undeniable.
With every being, I keep a unique
relationship.
And I see the agony within those who
stray from Me.
I am bound by strict nature.
Yet, I withhold great mercy!

8. Scrutiny of a Matriarch – My harsh reality:

I dare not hide My name
And Magdalene shall bear no shame
Forgiven what Eve has done
Abraham spares his son

A toast to Noah's Arc
As Calypso plays her part
A sword in Michael's hand
Four horsemen run the land

The guardian of black hole
Is keeper of the souls
A temper like no other
A highly pressured mother!

Forget not what is written
Or the apple that was bitten

But what lies in perfection
Is the notion of correction

Evolve

New beginnings are taking place. I shall reproduce with success to lead to a room full of strangers - as if it were already written.
I have extreme concern for the fate of my children. I presume it may be crucial that I save my children from even My own children.
I urge all to not overstep boundaries with Me.
For My calm expression could shadow a raging tsunami.

I feel it is My obligation to know the needs of the people.
It would be beneficial to have persons inform Me of those needs.

It is essential that I surround myself around those who are aware of My position on this earth. For you shall place no man above Me.
These persons shall leave judgment to Me.
I am quite fond of earth preservists. May they work to preserve this earth. And may they also put forth effort to refrain from the seven deadly sins
There should be a certain humble and respect for mothers.
So fairly, there shall be a certain humble and respect for Me.

I have walked amongst you. And I shall continue to do so. As I shall continue to document and update my findings. I maintain a list. And on this list, I shall continue to mark the names of those I come across.

I see your struggles. I know persecution.
I know natural birth. I know pain. I
know hardships. I know tragedy.
But I also know triumph, faith,
and trust.
No longer shall I feel the need to break
glass at the will of My anger!
No longer shall I ignore the gap
between mankind and Myself.
Have faith when I am here.
Have faith when my spirit remains.
Know my passion.
Know my power!
Know my mercy!
Know the depths of my love.

Respect My Vision.
And be wise in your dealings.
Govern your body and your temple.
And as I continue on this path, may all
men be made aware of Me.
For, man shall celebrate this new day

with grace!
For an enhancement has been gifted to mankind!
For I am here to create
My Kingdom,
My Paradise.

So shall it be!

www.ingramcontent.com/pod-product-compliance
Lightning Source LLC
LaVergne TN
LVHW021743060526
838200LV00052B/3449